MW01240633

Happiness Is Listening to Your Dog Snore

Humorous and Inspirational Dog Quotes to Celebrate Our Canine Friends

Untreed Reads

Happiness Is Listening to Your Dog Snore: Humorous and Inspirational Dog Quotes to Celebrate Our Canine Friends

Also available in ebook format.
Published by Untreed Reads, LLC
506 Kansas Street
San Francisco, CA 94107
www.untreedreads.com

Printed in the United States of America.

Introduction

It's said that a dog is the only one who will love you more than he loves himself. This collection of quotes and sayings, a mix of inspirational, quirky, sentimental, and downright funny, will remind readers of the best of times—time spent with dogs. The quotes range from well-known to those commonly seen on t-shirts. Contemporary authors, never at a loss for words, shared their thoughts as well.

May they bring sparks of memories and joy from dogs past, present, and future.

Dedicated to all who open their hearts and homes to the unconditional love of a dog.
There is no better friend.

Universal
Humor

I wonder what my
dog named me.

**My dog winks at me
sometimes. I always
wink back in case it's
some kind of code.**

Let's be honest.
If dogs could talk,
I'd have no need for people.

I'd love to,
but my dog said no.

**There is an
unwritten rule.
When your dog is
sleeping on you,
you don't move.**

I work hard so
my dog can have
nice things.

There's a 100% chance
I'd rather be home
with my dog.

**Dogs are furry little
children who will never
ask for money, a car, or
a phone.**

A woman cannot
survive on wine
alone. She also
needs a dog.

You don't get to tell
me what to do.
You're not my dog!

**My dog isn't spoiled. I'm
just well-trained.**

Yes, I know I got hair
on the couch.
That's why it's
called fur-niture.

When I yell at my dog
to stop barking, I wonder
if he's like, "This is awesome!
We are barking together."

You had me at Woof.

The person who
thinks dogs don't
talk just doesn't
want to learn a
second language.

Learn a lesson from your dog. No matter what life brings you, kick some grass over that shit and move on.

My dogs are the reason I wake up every morning. Really freaking early. Every. Single. Morning.

Live like someone left the gate open!

So far, our barking
has saved Mom and
Dad from murder: 40 mailmen,
16 UPS drivers, 3 Girl Scouts,
28 cats, and 1 sketchy-
looking plastic bag on the
road—and yet they remain
ungrateful.

**I don't always talk
about dogs.
Sometimes, I'm asleep.**

Love is in the air.
Wait, that's bacon.

Money can buy a
lot of things, but it
doesn't wiggle its
butt every time you
come in the door.

**Based on my wardrobe,
my favorite color is
dog hair.**

Your dog is the only one
who loves you even if
you haven't showered or
brushed your teeth
for three days.
Four days is pushing it.

Handle every situation
like a dog. If you can't
eat it or play with it,
pee on it and walk away.

**Dog: A personal stalker
who will follow you
wherever you go.
Bathroom included.**

In the event of a
tornado or other
natural disaster,
put salami or cheese
slices in your pocket
so the search and
rescue dogs find you first.

It was me.
I let the dogs out.

I don't want to adult today. I just want to dog. I'll be lying down on the floor in the sun; you can pet me and bring me some snacks.

I feel sorry for people who don't have dogs. I hear when they drop food on the floor, they have to pick it up themselves.

Taking a dog named
Shark to the beach
is a bad idea.

**I wanted to get a
German shepherd, but I
didn't want to learn
another language just
to have a dog.**

Today I saw a woman
talking to her cat. She
really thought the cat
understood. I told my
dog when I got home...
we both laughed and laughed.

Two fleas are coming out of a bar when one asks the other, "Do we take a dog or do we walk home?"

My windows aren't dirty. My dog is painting.

I need a belly rub.
I sit for treats.
—(Dog mottos)
Connie Berry, author

Real dog lovers just
swallow that random
hair in their coffee and
give you a steely gaze
while they're doing it.

**When your children are
teenagers, it's
important to have a dog
so someone in the house
is glad to see you.**

Yes, I know where your
socks are. I believe you
know where the treats are?
—Dog

Imagine a world where
dogs took bad owners
to the pound.

**Someday my kids will be
like, "Hey mom, can we
get another puppy?"
And I'm gonna be like,
"Heck, yeah, what a
great idea," and then
we'll have 76 dogs.**

Dogs are God's way
of apologizing for
your relatives.

There are just some
things my dogs do
for me that humans
can't. For instance,
dogs make me smile.
Humans make
my head hurt.

**My dog can't hear me
yelling at him to stop
chasing squirrels,
but he can hear a damn
cheese wrapper from
500 miles away.**

Sometimes losing
a pet is more painful
than losing a
human because
in the case of the
pet, you were not
pretending to love it.
—Amy Sedaris, author

**Some days you're
the dog; some days
you're the hydrant.**

I may seem quiet and reserved, but if you mess with my dogs, I will break out a level of crazy that will make your nightmares seem like a happy place.

Whoever said dogs aren't smart never tried to hide a Milk Bone from a Labrador.

You might wake
up next to the
wrong man...but
you'll never wake
up next to
the wrong dog.

—Judy Nedry, author

**I care deeply for about
five people in my life
and about 500 dogs
on the internet
I've never met.**

Dog snob: A person who would rather spend time with dogs than people.

If you want the best seat in the house, move the dog.

To a dog, the whole world is a smell.

When a dog wags her tail and barks at the same time, how do you know which end to believe?

The reason dogs have so many friends is because they wag their tails instead of their tongues.

If you don't like dogs, I don't like you. It's as simple as that.

A dog can express more with his tail in minutes than his owner can express with his tongue in hours.

We say we domesticated dogs. What really happened was, they domesticated us. What would make wolf dogs want to live with us? We have thumbs.

—Walt Boyes, author, editor, futurist

If it wasn't for puppies,
some people would never
go for a walk.

If you're uncomfortable
around my dog, I'm
happy to lock you
in the other room
when you come over.

**If aliens saw us
walking our dogs
and picking up their
poop, who would they
think is in charge?**

[Dogs] never talk
about themselves
but listen to you while
you talk about yourself
and keep up an appearance
of being interested in
the conversation.
—Jerome K. Jerome,
author, humorist

**To err is human—
to forgive, canine.**

I told my husband
before we got married,
"It's dogs or anti-
depressants. Pick one."
We have dogs.
—Ellen Byron, author

**It's not the size of
the dog in the fight,
it's the size of the
fight in the dog.**
—Mark Twain, author, humorist

If you get to thinkin'
you're a person of some influence,
try orderin'
somebody else's dog around.
—Cowboy Wisdom

**A well-trained dog
will make no attempt to
share your lunch. He will
just make you feel so
guilty that you cannot
enjoy it.**
—Helen Thomson, author

Home is where the
dog hair sticks to
everything but the dog.

Outside of a dog,
a book is a man's best
friend. Inside of a dog,
it's too dark to read.
—Groucho Marx, comedian

**What do dogs do on
their day off? Can't lie
around—that's their job.**
—George Carlin, comedian

Happiness is listening
to your dog snore.

If there are no dogs
in Heaven, then when
I die I want to go
where they went.
—Will Rogers, entertainer,
author, humorist

**The most affectionate
creature in the world
is a wet dog.**
—Charles Dickens, author

It was love at first
sight. I've finally found
my soulmutt.

Dogs don't shed.
They emit magical
fibers of love and joy.

**Dogs teach us a very
important lesson in life:
The mail man is
not to be trusted.**

—Sian Ford

My dog thinks
I'm a catch.

Breed Dog Quotes

BASSET HOUND

Live long and slobber.

BEAGLE

Darn it, I made eye contact. I'll just use my selective hearing excuse and run faster.

Beagles—trouble wrapped in cute.

I smell bacon! Three streets over, fifth house on the left.

BLOODHOUND

I'm awake. My face is still asleep, but I'm awake.

What kind of dog does Dracula have? A Bloodhound, of course.

BORDER COLLIE

Beware. My dog can't hold his licker.

I only know what I herd.

BOSTON TERRIER

I was normal until I got my
first Boston Terrier.

BOXER

I was just taking a
nap...and then...

BULLDOG

Bulldogs are like bowling balls of love rolling right straight down the alley at you and hoping for a strike.

To a Bulldog, the bigger the snore, the better the sleep.

CHIHUAHUA

Chihuahuas are the cheapest foot warmer you'll ever find.

If Chihuahuas ruled the world, it would never rain and there would always be a warm blanket to burrow under.

Chihuahuas prove the very best things sometimes come in tiny, ankle-biting packages.

CORGI

Life is short. So are my legs.

Depressed? Doctors prescribe a Corgi.

There ain't no butt like a Corgi butt.

I didn't fart. My butt blew you a bubble kiss.

DACHSHUND

The five-second rule when you drop food does not apply when you have a two-second Dachshund.

Dachshund: bravery of a lion, cunning of a fox, bark of a Doberman, body of a sausage.

Dachshund: half a dog high, a dog and a half long.

DALMATION

What does a Dalmatian say after dinner? Thanks, that really hit the spot.

FRENCH BULLDOG

Before you see what happened upstairs...I love you so much.

GOLDEN RETRIEVER

What do you call a smart
blond? A Golden Retriever.

**Something came in the
mail for you today.
Tasted important.**

GREAT DANE

No matter how big he is,
somehow a Great Dane will
find his way into his owner's
lap...or
the cat's bed.

HUSKY

Having a Husky is like a walk
in the park.
Jurassic Park.

IRISH SETTER

**Silence is golden unless
you have an Irish Setter.
Then silence is
suspicious.**

I was normal until two Irish
Setters ago.

JACK RUSSELL

I tried to be good, but
I got bored.

LABRADOR
RETRIEVER

**People without Labs
blame the dryer for
lost socks.**

I'm hungry. I haven't
had a snack for
five minutes!

MALAMUTE

NO! I am not a Husky.

PEKINGESE

I'm only talking to my
Pekingese today.

PITBULL

The Pitbull will always do what you ask of her, so be careful what you ask.

The only thing dangerous about a Pitbull is the human holding the leash.

POMERANIAN

Being cute is my job.

Pomeranians are potato chip dogs. You can't have just one.

POODLE

Resistance is futile. Obey the Poodle.

Poodle owner: (noun) Like a regular dog owner but cooler.

Poodles are like curly fries; you can't have just one.

PUG

Sometimes you just have to say, Pug it.

Why do I look so sad? Because I've found it gets me anything I want.

Get out of my way! I heard the fridge door open!

I run on Pug hair, coffee, and cuss words.

ROTTWEILER

I know this might be a bad time, but my water dish has been empty for five minutes now.

SCOTTIE

The food in my bowl does not smell like the food on your plate. Care to explain?

Whatever you think I did, I'm innocent.

SHIBA INU

Hold on. Okay, I'm not listening. Continue talking.

SHIH TZU

I don't give a Shih Tzu.

Being this cute must be so freaking ruff.

WEIMARANER

For Weimaraners, squirrels are
just tennis balls
thrown by God.

WESTIE

**West Highland White
Terrier, aka Westie—
small dog, big attitude.**

I'm not addicted to Westies.
We're just in a very committed
relationship.

YORKIE

I don't always bark at night
but when I do, it's
for no reason.

**Really, two Yorkies are
better than one. Three
would be ideal but four
are just as easy. Might
as well have five.**

Inspirational

A dog is one of the
few things in life
that is exactly what
it seems.

**When the world around
me is going crazy, and
I'm losing faith in
humanity, I just have to
take one look at my
dog to know that good
still exists.**

The best therapist
has fur and four legs.

My dog is my heart.

**Bliss is the result of
a silent conversation
between me
and my dog.**

The first dog is the dog
who gives you so much
that the first dog is
often the reason for
the second dog.

God is the source of
unconditional love.
Or my dog.
—Connie Berry, author

**It is impossible
to keep a straight
face in the presence
of one or more puppies.**

Dogs awaken happiness.

Buy a pup, and your money
will buy love unflinching.
—Rudyard Kipling, author

**You can always find
hope in a dog's eyes.**

All dogs are
therapy dogs.
The majority of
them are just
freelancing.

The best thing about dogs is, if you're celebrating, they start celebrating too. They don't have to know why— they are always ready for good news and a party!

Dogs are like chocolate—they can ease your stress at the end of a hard day and they bring sweetness into your life.

—Margaret Mizushima, author

Dogs know the
difference between
a connecting
touch and a
correcting touch.
—Mary Debono, Feldenkrais
practitioner, author

**Dogs can't hide joy.
They "smile"
from both ends.**
—Amy Shojai, author

Life is too short to just have one dog.

A dog reflects the family life. Whoever saw a frisky dog in a gloomy family, or a sad dog in a happy one? Snarling people have snarling dogs, dangerous people have dangerous ones.

—Sir Arthur Conan Doyle, author

Rescued is my
favorite breed.

I would recommend to
those persons who are
inclined to stagnate,
whose blood is
beginning to thicken
sluggishly in their veins,
to try keeping four
dogs, two of which are
puppies.

—Elizabeth von Arnim, author

Man himself cannot
express love and humility
by external signs so
plainly as does a
dog when, with
drooping ears, hanging
lips, flexuous body, and
wagging tail, he meets
his beloved master.
—Charles Darwin,
naturalist, author

**A dog is nothing
but a furry person.**

No one appreciates the very special genius of your conversation as much as the dog does.

—Christopher Morley, journalist, author, poet

No man can be condemned for owning a dog. As long as he has a dog, he has a friend.

—Will Rogers, entertainer, author, humorist

The kindness lavished
on dogs, if evenly
distributed, would
establish peace on earth.
—William Feather,
publisher, author

**The kindness one does
for one animal may not
change the world, but it
will change the world of
that one animal.**

Live. Laugh. Bark.

If a dog will not come to you after having looked you in the face, you should go home and examine your conscience.

—Woodrow Wilson, 28th President of the United States

Dogs are the best example of a being who doesn't need to lie to protect someone's pride.

—Ammiel Josiah Monterde, author

A lot of shelter dogs
are mutts like me.
—Barack Obama, 44th
President of the United States

**When you feel lousy,
puppy therapy is
indicated.**
—Sara Paretsky, author

Life is a series of dogs.
—George Carlin, comedian

Secondhand animals make
first-class pets.

**The average dog is
nicer than the
average person.**
—Andy Rooney, radio
and TV personality

Dogs come in all shapes,
sizes, and colors.
But their hearts are
all the same. Full of love.

Some people will never
understand how much
I love my dog. But that's
okay. My dog knows!

**If you're lucky,
a dog will come
into your life, steal
your heart, and
change everything.**

Do you ever look at
your dog and think,
"How did I get so lucky?"

Dogs are God's way
of showing us
He didn't want us to
walk alone.

Dogs come into our lives
to teach us about love;
they depart to teach us
about loss. A new dog
never replaces an old
dog. It merely expands
the heart.

Not Carnegie, Vanderbilt, and Astor together could have raised money enough to buy a quarter share in my little dog.

—Ernest Thompson Seton, author, wildlife artist

Does not the gratitude of the dog put to shame any man who is ungrateful to his benefactors?

—Saint Basil, theologian

My dog does this amazing thing where he just exists and makes my life better because of it.

The gift which I am sending you is called a dog, and is in fact the most precious and valuable possession of mankind.

—Theodorus Gaza,
humanist,
translator of Aristotle

The absolutely one
unselfish friend
that man can
have in this selfish
world, the one that
never deserts him,
the one that never
proves ungrateful
or treacherous,
is his dog.

—George Graham Vest

Sentimental

Dogs are the
twinkle in God's eyes.
—Kylie Logan, author

**For any skeptics
out there, dogs are
living proof that
miracles do exist.**

If Heaven doesn't
have dogs, St. Peter
can just direct me
to the Rainbow Bridge.

I love all dogs, but
there's nothing like
the sweet, gentle soul
of an old dog.

**Adorable I am,
give me treats you
must.**

How is it that Chet, narrator of the Chet and Bernie series, and therefore a figment of my imagination, has taught me a lot about life? In some sense, he must be real.

—Spencer Quinn, author

It came to me that every time I lose a dog, they take a piece of my heart with them, and every new dog who comes into my life gifts me with a piece of their heart. If I live long enough, all the components of my heart will be dog, and I will become as generous and loving as they are.

Beware of the Dog.
He will steal your heart.

Those who teach us the most about humanity aren't always human.

Without my dog,
my wallet would be
full and my house
would be clean,
but my heart
would be empty.

Every once in a while,
a dog enters your life
and changes everything.

**Happiness starts
with a wet nose
and ends with a tail.**

If the kindest souls
were rewarded with
the longest lives, dogs
would outlive us all.

Friendship isn't about whom you've known the longest but who came and never left your side.

Dog. A noun. Definition: the best friend you will ever have.

From the first moment Lily
tilted her head when I spoke
to her and looked at me with
those big brown eyes, she
owned me. Lily walks me, feeds
my soul, teaches me about
love, playfulness, and
how to just be.
—Sherry Harris, author

The best part of having a dog is seeing the pure love and loyalty in those brown eyes, the joy of being with you, whether it's tossing a ball in the rear yard, or going for a drive to the grocery store, or just sharing a couch. The hardest part of having a dog is trying to be worthy of this utter devotion.

—Brendan DuBois, author

Too many people miss out on what we can learn from dogs. Once they trust, they love completely and fiercely, protect those they love, forgive others for their faults, and are totally themselves, without shame or embarrassment. If you are blessed enough to live with a dog, observe, and never for a moment let the love they shower upon you be left unreturned.

—Eric Schumacher, actor/filmmaker

Dogs don't need long
to achieve perfection.
Most of them are
born that way.
—Joy Ward, author

I asked a kid,
"What is love?"
He answered, "Love
is when a puppy
licks your face."
I laughed before
he added,
"even when you
left him alone all day."

The dog was created
specifically for children.
He is the god of frolic.
—Henry Ward Beecher, American
Congregationalist clergyman

**If you don't believe dogs
have souls, you haven't
looked into their eyes
long enough.**

Love is a four-legged word.

My goal in life is to
be as good of a person
as my dog already
thinks I am.

**My sunshine doesn't
come from the skies. It
comes from the love
that's in my dog's eyes.**

Keep calm and
pet a dog.

Having a dog will bless you with the happiest days of your life and one of the worst days.

What a beautiful world it would be if humans had hearts like dogs.

A dog may be man's best friend, but a child's best friend is a puppy.

The dog lives for
the day, the hour,
even the moment.
—Robert Falcon Scott, explorer

**I am thankful
for my pets
because they
complete my family.**

Best part of the day
is coming home to a
wagging tail.

who loves me
will love my dog also.
—Proverb

**Old age means
realizing you will
never own all the
dogs you wanted to.**
—Joe Gores, author, screenwriter

A dog has the soul
of a philosopher.
—Plato, philosopher

There are no bad
days when you
come home to
a dog's love.

**The bond with a true
dog is as lasting as the
ties of this earth
will ever be.**
—Konrad Lorenz, zoologist,
ethologist, ornithologist

Home is where
the dog runs
to greet you.

Animals share
with us the privilege
of having a soul.
—Pythagoras, philosopher

**If a man aspires
towards a righteous
life, his first act of
abstinence is from
injury to animals.**
—Albert Einstein, physicist

Some things just
fill your heart
with trying.

You haven't appreciated friendship until you've felt the love of a dog.

Histories are more full of examples of the fidelity of dogs than of friends.

—Alexander Pope, poet

Every dog deserves a home, but not every home deserves a dog.

The better I get
to know men, the
more I find myself
loving dogs.
—Charles De Gaulle, former
President of France

**A dog judges others
not by their color or
creed or class but by
who they are inside.**

A true friend leaves
paw prints on your heart.

Dogs teach us
a lot of things
but none more
important than
to love unconditionally.

**A dog might destroy
your shoes but will
never willingly break
your heart.**

Whoever said that
diamonds are a
girl's best friend
never owned a dog.

**If you eliminate
smoking and gambling,
you will be amazed to
find that almost all an
Englishman's pleasures
can be, and mostly are,
shared by his dog.**

—George Bernard Shaw,
playwright

I care not for a
man's religion whose
dog and cat are not
the better for it.
—Abraham Lincoln, 16th
President of the United States

**As grateful as I am
for every day you have
left, I will always
want one more.**

When all else fails,
just pet your dog.

Dogs' lives are
too short. Their
only fault, really.
—Agnes Sligh Turnbull, author

**Sometimes we
put our great
treasure in museums.
Other times we
take them for walks.**

The truth is that
it's just really hard
for me to get to
sleep without a dog
in my bedroom.
—Jimmy Stewart, actor

Dogs are small
rays of light,
caught on Earth
for a short time,
to brighten our days.

Kindly the father said to him, "I've left you to the end. I've turned my own name around, and have called you Dog, my friend."

The road to my
heart is paved
with pawprints.

**The greatest pleasure of
a dog is that you may
make a fool of yourself
with him and not only
will he not scold you,
but he will make a fool
of himself too.**

—Samuel Butler, author

When I needed a hand,
I found your paw.

There is no
greater earthly
privilege than to
have been loved
by a dog.

**Dogs are small rays
of light, caught
on Earth for
a short time, to
brighten our days.**

Those who love dogs,
know something
about God.
—Fakeer Ishavardas,
metaphysical poet

**My little dog—
a heartbeat
at my feet.**
—Edith Wharton, author

Until one has loved
an animal, a part of
one's soul remains
unawakened.
—Anatole France, poet

I think dogs are
the most amazing
creatures. They give
unconditional love.
For me they are the
role model for being alive.
—Gilda Radner, comedian, actor

**In order to really enjoy
a dog, one doesn't
merely try to train him
to be semi human.
The point of it is to
open oneself to the
possibility of
becoming partly a dog.**
—Edward Hoagland, author

You think dogs will
not be in heaven?
I tell you, they will
be there long before
any of us.
—Robert Louis Stevenson, author

**The dog has got more
fun out of man than
man has got out of the
dog, for man is the
more laughable of the
two animals.**

—James Thurber,
cartoonist, author

Let sleeping dogs lie.
—Robert Walpole, first Prime
Minister of Great Britain

Pets are like infants that never grow up. Forever children. We love them for that.

Dogs laugh, but they
laugh with their tails.
—Max Eastman,
writer, poet, activist

The problem with loving dogs is that you outlive all but the last one.

—Edward Grinnan

There are three faithful friends: an old wife, an old dog, and ready money.

—Benjamin Franklin, scientist, inventor, statesman

Little pup, big world.

**Dogs are our guides
through life. They
reflect the highest and
the best humans
can become.**
—Joy Ward, author

And so, the snuggles
and treats begin.

Dogs wait for us
patiently and faithfully.

**Everyone thinks
they have the
best dog, and none
of them are wrong.**

Not every person knows
how to love a dog,
but every dog knows
how to love a person!

Quotes by Untreed Reads Authors

"Woof."
—Michael Bracken, editor and
author of over 1,500 short stories,
when asked for a "dog quote,"
rather than a
"quote about dogs."

I was told to pick the biggest pup from the litter. When you do that, you get a 90-pound Golden. Our retriever, Cory, was clumsy and hated water. She would have made a terrible retriever, but she made a wonderful family dog. Who says dogs can't spell? We started spelling w-a-l-k when we were thinking of taking her on a "you-know-what." She learned both to spell w-a-l-k AND the meaning of "you-know-what."

—Kaye George, author of the People in the Wind mysteries

Dogs are better than apples
at keeping the doctor away.
And anybody else without a
handy box of treats.
—Jeanne DuBois, author of
"Wooden Ships," in *Peace, Love,
and Crime: Crime Fiction Inspired by
Songs of the '60s*

We had a dog, Tessa, the only dog I've ever not been violently, go-to-the-ER allergic to. My wife Laurie always said Tessa wasn't really a dog, but a little old Jewish man in a dog suit.

—Josh Pachter, author and editor, *The Beat of Black Wings: Crime Fiction Inspired by the Songs of Joni Mitchell*

Choose a puppy,
choose a friend.
Choose a kitten,
choose a critic.
—Karen Keeley, author of
"Bloody, Just Bloody Lovely" in
*Peace, Love, and Crime: Crime
Fiction Inspired by Songs of the '60s*

It must be wonderful to be a dog. You get to eat off the floor, stop every day to sniff the roses—and poles, fire hydrants, and crotches—and you are petted all the time without ever having to return the favor.

—Barb Goffman, short story author and editor

Every dog wants
to be a hero.
—Robin F. Gainey, *Jack of Hearts*

**Any homeless dog who's
ever chased a rabbit
knows that woes fade in
the face of exhilaration.**
—Robin F. Gainey, *Jack of Hearts*

One could never
judge a dog
by its collar.
—Robin F. Gainey, *Jack of Hearts*

**Dogs never pass up the
opportunity to have fun.
It is the very heart of
every living spirit, the
essence of every dog.
It encourages strong
bonds and
deep affection.**
—Robin F. Gainey, *Jack of Hearts*

Dog wrote the
book on
faithfulness.
—Robin F. Gainey, *Jack of Hearts*

**Dogs are
philanthropists.
They never pass up
an opportunity
to give.**
—Robin F. Gainey, *Jack of Hearts*

These days, Good-dog
was my middle name.
—Robin F. Gainey, *Jack of Hearts*

I knew that a noble dog's
duty was to gild the
human spirit.

—Robin F. Gainey, *Jack of Hearts*

**The scent of Roman
mornings was designed
for dogs.**

—Robin F. Gainey, *Jack of Hearts*

I don't actually have a dog or dogs of my own. I am lazy, so I rely on loaner dogs—dogs who belong to friends or family. Which is normally great because I can have all the fun and give them back when we're tired. But during the quarantine, it didn't work out so well. I could do phone calls and Zoom with family and friends, but the dogs missed me. You should have seen how excited they were to see me again, after months apart.

—Donna Andrews, author of "Night at the Opera" in *Monkey Business: Crime Fiction Inspired by the Films of the Marx Brothers*

When you're desperate for comfort, nothing beats the tail-wagging joy of a dog who thinks you are the center of the universe. In that moment, you are.

—Wendy Harrison, author of "Nights in White Satin" in *Peace, Love, and Crime: Crime Fiction Inspired by Songs of the '60s*

It may be that dogs have a greater ability to make friends than humans do.

Horses and dogs often become quite friendly with one another. Dogs will even make friends with burros. An Australian shepherd by the name of Jellybean grew up with a burro named Nicholas. The burro would call out early in the morning, a noise that sounded like an old car horn honking. The dog would race over to the pasture where the burro slept, jump the fence, and join his friend for their first walk of the day. When night fell, the dog would jump up on the burro's back, and the two would go to sleep under the quiet, star-studded desert sky.

—Jeffrey Moussaieff Masson, *Dogs Have the Strangest Friends*

One dog in the lap
is worth two peeing
in the bush.
—Kari Wainwright, author of
"Drunk Raisins," in the anthology
*The Killer Wore Cranberry: A Sixth
Scandalous Serving*

Dogs have purer souls.
They love unconditionally.
We call it "doglike devotion."
But it's only love in its
purest form.
—Edith Layton, *An Enchanting Regency Christmas*

But in truth, he felt humbled and shocked by the dog's devotion— and staggered at how the mere fact of her loyalty gave him joy.
—Edith Layton, *An Enchanting Regency Christmas*

Made in the USA
Middletown, DE
29 December 2022